Entrepreneurs' Guide to Social Media Customer Service

Table of Contents

We don't have a choice on whether we DO social media, the question is how well we DO it.

Chapter 1. Introduction

In the vibrant world of entrepreneurship, where the success of business hinges not only on what is sold but also how it is communicated, understanding an effective Social Media Customer Service strategy is paramount. Unveil the secret to nurturing irreplaceable customer relationships in our compelling Special Report, 'Entrepreneurs' Guide to Social Media Customer Service'. This report, brimming with expert insights, practical advice, and real-world examples, will empower you to transform your social media presence into a thriving hub of engagement and satisfaction. If you're seeking ways to increase customer loyalty, resolve issues swiftly and creatively, or leverage negative comments into positive changes, let this be the actionable blueprint to propel your business vision forward. Jump into this refreshing journey, and give your venture the competitive edge it deserves!

Chapter 2. Understanding the Role of Social Media in Customer Service

In an era where digital interactions dominate the consumer landscape, social media platforms have assumed a pivotal role in establishing robust customer service dynamics. It is essential to understand that social media, with its vast reach and instantaneous feedback mechanisms, is significantly more than a mere marketing tool. It's a vibrant avenue for customer service where queries can be responded to, issues resolved, and feedback sought in real-time.

2.1. The Evolution of Social Media as a Customer Service Platform

Historically, customer service was rooted in face-to-face interactions and phone calls, often leading to time-consuming resolution processes and limited feedback channels. The digital revolution, however, significantly transformed this narrative. Social media emerged as a potent platform where customer queries could be effortlessly routed and promptly addressed. Consequently, businesses have recognized it as a viable medium of customer service, deserving of as much strategic consideration as traditional channels.

Digital customer service strategies, such as social listening, sentiment analysis and direct messaging, have seen brands calibrate their interactions to match their customer expectations better. The capability to facilitate open dialogues, deliver personalized responses and obtain genuine feedback has resulted in social media platforms becoming an indispensable component of an effective customer service model.

2.2. Realizing the Power of Social Media in Customer Relations

Social media is a two-way communication medium that breaks down barriers between organizations and their patrons. It fosters trust and facilitates candid conversations around points of dissatisfaction, queries, and compliments. Its criticality is showcased in its dual role - as a crisis management tool and a proactive platform for ensuring customer satisfaction.

To begin with, customers increasingly vie for personalized attention and instant problem resolution. Social media provides the ideal platform to cater to this demand, strengthening the overall customer-brand relationship. Directing resources to handle queries or issues on social platforms can lead to faster turnaround times, immediate responses, and a more satisfactory resolution process.

Further, it plays an invaluable role in crisis management. When an issue spirals, social media helps control the narrative by responding directly to customer complaints and taking immediate action to rectify the problem, thereby mitigating damages to the brand's reputation.

2.3. The Interplay of Social Media Platforms in Customer Service

Not all social media platforms are created equal, and hence it becomes crucial to understand the nuances and strengths of various platforms to tailor your customer service delivery.

1. Twitter: With its character restriction, Twitter is apt for quick and concise customer interactions. The platform's public nature also means an excellent service can generate positive branding, while any negative incident may quickly escalate.

2. Facebook: A platform boasting diverse demographic usage, Facebook is suited for comprehensive conversations involving more complex concerns. Its capability to support multimedia and long-form content allows businesses to interact more deeply with customers.

3. Instagram: A visually driven platform, Instagram is an excellent place to showcase your brand and engage in visual storytelling. While it lacks the depth for detailed problem-solving, quick responses via comments or direct messages can be effective.

4. LinkedIn: As a professional networking site, LinkedIn is ideal for B2B customer service interactions and professional updates.

Understanding these dynamics can substantially streamline your social media customer service strategy and ensure maximum return on investment.

2.4. Harnessing Social Media for Superior Customer Service

Successful social media customer service is not just about responding to queries or resolving complaints; it's about leveraging the platform's potential to build strong customer relationships.

1. Quick Response Times: Responsiveness is key on social media platforms. Quick and informative replies not only satisfy a customer's immediate need but also demonstrate a commitment to customer service.

2. Feedback Collection: Social media, with its interactive capabilities, is a treasure trove of customer opinion. Actively solicit feedback, respond constructively to critical reviews, and display a genuine willingness to improve.

3. Personalized Interactions: The beauty of social media lies in its ability to forge personal connections. Addressing customers by

their names, using a personalized tone, and showing empathy can make customers feel valued.

4. Crisis Management: Adopt a proactive approach in situations which could potentially damage your brand's reputation. Swift acknowledgment of the issue, followed by diligent efforts to rectify it, can prevent negative sentiment from escalating.

5. Monitor and Evaluate: Use specific monitoring tools and analytics to measure your performance. This data will help you understand the effectiveness of your strategies and identify areas needing improvement.

Understanding the role of social media in customer service is a task that requires diligent attention and strategic planning. The power of social media to build or damage a brand's reputation is immense and, much like the weather, it can change very rapidly. But on harnessing its full strength, businesses can create a customer service experience that facilitates connection, fostips loyalty, and ultimately drives growth. This vibrant, intricate world awaits the canny business entrepreneur who is willing to delve deeper and unearth its many possibilities in the realm of customer service.

Chapter 3. The Art of Listening: Monitoring Social Media for Customer Feedback

In today's interconnected world, entrepreneurs are increasingly tapping into the vast potential peer-to-peer communication offers, in particular, leveraging on social media's widespread influence. By monitoring social media for customer feedback, businesses can forge strong bonds with their customers – but how exactly does one go about this task, and how can they do it well?

3.1. The Importance of Active Listening on Social Media

Active listening is an essential strategy for nurturing a positive relationship with customers and building a loyal clientele base. But in the realm of the Internet, it means more than just hearing - it involves a thorough assessment of customer feedback shared on social media platforms, interpreting these observations, and taking the necessary actions to address concerns or applaud appreciations effectively.

Active social media monitoring facilitates improved understanding of customers' needs, identifies possible toolkits for improved service delivery, and enhances the overall marketing strategy of the business. It offers an interactive peek into the very hearts and minds of your customers – it's a digital treasure trove of insights waiting to be explored.

3.2. Monitoring Techniques & Tools

To harvest this wealth of information efficiently, it's essential to equip oneself with suitable tools and platforms designed accurately for this task. These tools act as each entrepreneur's digital ears, listening in to consumer sentiment expressed across various platforms. Here are some that prove handy:

- Hootsuite: A comprehensive tool with functionalities for scheduling posts, responding to messages and comments, and, importantly, listening to relevant conversations on social media.

- Sprout Social: Offering similar capabilities as Hootsuite, Sprout Social also includes an analytics dashboard to dissect and interpret social media conversations.

- Mention: This platform scans millions of sources in real-time, enabling businesses to monitor mentions of their brand, competitors, and keywords related to their industry.

- TweetDeck: Twitter-centric monitoring tool ideal for tracking conversations, mentions, hashtags specific to the Twitterverse.

These tools scour social media platforms, blogs, news sites, and forums for specific keywords, phrases, or brand mentions, spelling out what is being said about your business online, in real-time. Deciphering these conversations is thus crucial for responding accurately and promptly.

3.3. Deciphering the Conversation

Once you have your ear to the ground, the next step is understanding the conversations the digital public sphere echoes with. There are several components to be aware of:

Similar to a detective's intuition, entrepreneurs need to grasp subjectivity and urgency. Subjectivity pertains to whether the comment is objective (based on fact) or subjective (based on opinion) and urgency relates to the immediacy of a required response.

While all feedback is crucial, negative comments should be prioritized due to their potential implication on a brand's reputation if left unattended. Neutral comments, on the other hand, can be turned positive with a thoughtful, personalized response, whereas positive comments warrant acknowledgment and appreciation.

3.4. Components of Effective Response

A good response strategy on social media hinges on three key components: timeliness, empathy, and actionability. Responding swiftly to comments shows customers that their feedback is valued. Empathy lets them know they've been understood, and actionability assures them that their issue will be resolved—these crucial elements foster longevity in customer relationships and enhances brand reputation.

3.5. Monitoring to Inform Business Strategies

Regular social media monitoring is not only beneficial for resolving customer issues but also strategically fuels their business objectives. Analyzing feedback patterns can help understand customer needs and preferences, market trends, and the competitive landscape, molding the entrepreneurial vision according to the real-world business climate.

Conclusively, the art of listening on social media is a nuanced dance, a delicate interplay of many factors. By optimizing their monitoring strategy and making the most of the digital platforms available, entrepreneurs can enhance their customer service delivery, build robust relationships with customers, and strategically navigate their business in today's digital-dominated world.

Chapter 4. Crafting Impactful Responses: Thriving in the Public Eye

Crafting impactful responses in the realm of social media customer service is not merely about answering enquiries or resolving issues; it catapults far beyond that. It involves molding your company's voice, showcasing empathy, and fostering a cordial relationship with customers, all while under the public eye's intense scrutiny. It structures your brand's public image and sets the bar for how your audience perceives you. This part of the report explicates the importance of producing significant responses in social media interactions and bestows upon you proven strategies and systems to excel in this domain.

4.1. Becoming the Voice of Your Brand

As soon as you respond to a customer query or feedback on social media, you instantly become the voice of your brand. It is important to remember that your responses are not just a reflection of your customer service approach, but also the brand's persona, value, and ethos. Understanding, framing, and religiously practicing the tone that fits your brand personality, whether empathetical, playful, professional, cheeky, or a blend of these elements, is key to establishing or reinforcing the desired brand image. You want your customers to feel a connection with your responses, to resonate with your brand's voice, and, most importantly, to believe that the brand cares about them. A thorough understanding of your brand, audience, and their language, cultural subtleties, and preferences should guide the overall tone and content of your responses.

4.2. Utilizing Personalized and Empathetic Responses

Social media has brought brands and their customers closer than ever before. Customers, nowadays, crave personalized attention and demand it from social media interactions as much as, if not more than, in-person interactions. Crafting responses that address the customer by their first name and demonstrate a clear understanding of their unique situation and feelings can prove monumentally beneficial. They convey the message that every customer is valuable, and their experience matters. Empathy, expressed through phrases like 'we understand', 'we can imagine', 'we're really sorry', can help you connect with your customers on a more personal and emotional level, and helps to build trust in your brand.

4.3. Mastering the Art of Speedy Responses

In the social media universe, timeliness is crucial. Customers expect and appreciate speedy responses. Delayed replies run the risk of infuriating customers and can even prompt them to share their negative experiences publicly, tarnishing your brand's reputation. Implementing a robust system that ensures swift responses, even during non-business hours, is imperative. Various tech tools, including AI-powered bots, can assist with quick, albeit personalized, initial responses, reassuring the customers that their voice has been heard.

4.4. Dealing with Negative Comments Gracefully

Negative comments are inevitable in the social media environment.

Transforming these potential threats into opportunities to showcase your brand's commitment to customer satisfaction is a crucial aspect of effective social media customer service. First and foremost, it's necessary to acknowledge the issue and express sincere apologies. Defensive or provocative responses can deepen the issue and cause further damage. Instead, attempt to move the conversation to a private channel like direct messages (DMs) or emails. This approach reduces public display of the problem while showing the customer that you are committed to resolving their issue.

4.5. Crafting Compelling Responses for Public Enquiries

Public enquiries require tactful handling as they can significantly affect your brand's public image. They are opportunities to showcase your brand's value, commitment to customer satisfaction, and your ability to provide clear and concise information. Responding quickly, using easy-to-understand language with a touch of your brand's personality, addressing the user's concern explicitly, and offering an actionable solution form the crux of an impactful public enquiry response.

4.6. Navigating Crisis Situations

Crisis situations, such as a barrage of negative comments or a public callout, require a blend of patience, empathy, and assertiveness. They are opportunities to turn a potential PR disaster into a testament of your brand's resilience and commitment to its customers. Craft your responses with utmost care, aiming to defuse the situation rather than kindling it. Ensure your message is cohesive and consistent across all platforms. Address the issue head-on, apologize where necessary, and communicate the actions your company is taking to resolve the problem and prevent its recurrence.

Crafting impactful responses, while challenging, can strengthen your relationship with customers and help you thrive in the public eye. Always remember, it's not just about saying the right thing but saying it in the right way, at the right time, and in the right place. These strategies, when executed correctly, can empower your brand to build irreplaceable customer relationships, maintain a sterling reputation, and ensure sustainable success in your social media customer service endeavors.

Chapter 5. Turning Challenges into Opportunities: Handling Negative Feedback

Ironically, embracing negative feedback tends to generate far more optimal results than avoiding it. This transformation begins by adopting a constructive outlook where complaints are viewed as gateways rather than barriers. This chapter delves into the manifold aspects of handling adverse customer reactions and maneuvers them into catalysts for unprecedented growth and insight.

5.1. The Opportunity in Negative Feedback

Some entrepreneurs might wince at the thought of negative feedback from customers making its way into the public domain. However, if approached constructively, these sentiments can become incredible opportunities to better comprehend your customer's needs, weaknesses within your operations, and potential avenues for improvement.

Understanding customer distress is the first step towards transforming adversity into a springboard for progress. It is these instances of negative feedback that provide a mirror to your business operations, reflecting those elements that may need polishing. It forces you to ask questions like, What part of the customer experience incited dissatisfaction? Where did things go wrong? How can this be avoided in the future? By seeking answers to these questions, negative feedback can help identify key areas for improvement and, subsequently, improve overall customer satisfaction.

5.2. The Power of a Well-crafted Response

Creating an impactful counter-response is a pivotal aspect of handling negative reviews or comments. Begin with empathy - acknowledging and validating the customer's concerns and feelings. A simple "We understand your frustration and we apologize for any inconvenience caused." can diffuse tension and set the stage for a more productive conversation.

Clarify any misunderstandings, providing accurate information where necessary. If a mistake has occurred from your end, hold up your hands, admit it, and reassure the customer that the necessary measures will be instituted to prevent its future recurrence. A forward-looking stance focusing more on solutions rather than a rhetoric of regret is essential for winning back disgruntled customers.

5.3. Customer Retention After a Mistake

Mistakes can sometimes feel like a setback for any business, particularly when they are played out in the public sphere. However, the impact of a mistake can be substantially softened with proactive and effective customer service. A candid conversation might lead to not just a salvaged relationship, but an even stronger one, anchored in a newfound trust in your transparency and commitment to making things right.

Several studies show that customers who had a bad experience, followed by an exceptionally good recovery interaction, are more likely to be loyal, repeat customers than those who never had a problem in the first place. This adds a fresh dimension to encountering blunders and their subsequent handling - they can potentially serve as powerful customer loyalty builders.

5.4. Harnessing Public Platforms

Negative comments are most poignant when aired on public networks, creating a ripple effect far more extensive than individual conversations. However, this is a double-edged sword. By handling criticism effectively and professionally in the public sphere through social media platforms, you are not only resolving the issue at hand but also communicating very powerfully to other potential customers.

Your response to negative feedback is, therefore, not just for the disappointed customer, but for every potential customer who may view that interaction. This can relay a strong message about your commitment to customer satisfaction, turning a negative situation into a testimonial to your product and service quality.

5.5. Turning Detractors into Promoters

The most powerful part of handling a negative feedback scenario is the potential to convert dissatisfied customers, or 'detractors,' into strong advocates or 'promoters.' By handling a complaint effectively and rectifying issues swiftly, you can often change a customer's opinion about your brand or business. The former critics might end up praising your commitment to customer service, thereby reinforcing your company's reputation, product quality, and ultimately earning high appraisals from the previously disgruntled consumer.

Negative feedback can sting, no doubt about it. But it's how you react to it - and what you learn from it - that can potentially turn a dissatisfied consumer into a brand ambassador and use that criticism as a potent force for your venture's continual refinement. With an empathetic response, public transparency, a solution-oriented approach, and an unwavering commitment to improvement, critics can become allies, pushing the boundaries of your business into expanding fields of customer delight.

Chapter 6. Establishing and Upholding Your Digital Customer Service Etiquette

In an era where digital interactions hold significant sway over customer impressions, establishing a robust digital customer service etiquette is a feat of cardinal importance. Companies that navigate this intricate voyage with finesse and tact catechize an unspoken covenant of trust, engender a sense of belonging and foster loyalty among customers. This, in turn, exerts a ripple effect, culminating in improved brand image, elevated customer satisfaction, enhanced word-of-mouth marketing and thus, bolstered business performance.

6.1. The Paradigm of Digital Customer Service Etiquette

Digital customer service etiquette underpins the tenors of conduct that service professionals should embody while interacting via digital media. It defines a set of values, behaviors and communication styles that resonate with respect, empathy, transparency, and professionalism. In an analogous vein to offline manners, this etiquette ensures that customers receive consistent and respectful service across digital mediums, instilling in them a sense of value and authenticity that is germane to fostering enduring relationships.

6.2. Comprehending the Digital Customer

Given the eclectic span of digital platforms - from social media platforms to company websites and email interactions - customers' expectations have evolved in tandem. The digital customer craves immediacy, simplicity, and a personalized approach while they interact. Contextualizing customer expectations, comprehending their psyche and aligning your service etiquette therewith is of the essence.

Companies should strive to make their services accessible across multiple digital touchpoints, promptly respond to queries, personalize communication with customer's name and prior interaction history. Moreover, they should moderate conversations with courtesy, maintaining an optimal balance between formality and friendliness, without resorting to technical jargon.

6.3. Cultivating Empathy in Digital Interactions

Empathy, although a quintessential human quality, is powerfully transformative in digital customer service. By approaching conversations with empathy, companies can facilitate a deep-seated emotional connection and harbor customer trust. However, displaying empathy in digital interactions that lack non-verbal cues is a challenge. Businesses can overcome this by attentive listening, personalized acknowledgments, using an empathetic language tone and proactively catering to anticipated needs.

6.4. Upholding Transparency

Transparency is a linchpin in cultivating trust and authenticity. While transparency isn't about revealing every corporate mystery, it does center around honesty in communication, particularly during service lapses. Apprising customers honestly about issues, the steps undertaken to resolve them, and the timeline for resolution will cultivate their patience and understanding.

6.5. The Role of Apologies in Digital Customer Service Etiquette

A well-articulated apology can spin a negative impression into a positive affirmation of your commitment towards customer satisfaction. However, while the art of apologizing is essential, it's equally crucial to accompany it with swift and concrete problem resolution actions.

6.6. Preserving Professionalism

Exhibiting professionalism in digital interactions underscores the credibility of your customer service. Professional customer service ensures punctual responses, cohesive and clear communication, respect for customer's time and problem, self-control in heated situations and owning up to mistakes rather than shifting blame.

6.7. The Confluence of Etiquette and Automation

Automated customer service, when judiciously deployed, can revolutionize customer service efficiency and responsiveness. However, it's also equally imperative not to depersonalize the customer service experience in the name of automation. 'Phonic' sentences, tailored automatic replies, chatbots with personalized greetings can bring human-like warmth to automated interactions.

In conclusion, mastering digital customer service etiquette necessitates a mixture of empathy, professionalism, accessibility, transparency, personalization, and well-maneuvered automation. Embrace these golden rules of digital etiquette, nurture priceless customer relationships, and watch your business scale new heights!

Chapter 7. Building Trust Online: Transparency and Authenticity

Building trust online is a multi-faceted endeavor that operates within the framework of transparency and authenticity — two key principles in contemporary digital customer service practices. The cultivation of these principles is critical for fostering robust customer relationships, facilitating loyalty, and ultimately, advocating for your brand in the hyper-competitive social media spectrum. In this in-depth exploration, we will dissect the practical and theoretical aspects of building online trust, sharing insights into how businesses can establish and maintain a deeply transparent and authentically engaging digital presence.

7.1. The Imperative of Online Trust

In the digital landscape of entrepreneurship, trust can be perceived as an invisible currency – a deposit made by businesses into the accounts of their customers, fostering faith, loyalty, and ongoing patronage. The dynamics of online trust are complex and multidimensional, relying heavily on a business's capacity to uphold transparency and authenticity in its interactions.

Transparency, in an organizational context, refers to the deliberate act of openness, communication, and accountability. It is the prerequisite for open dialogue with customers, acknowledging successes, and openly admitting and correcting failures. An approach committed to transparency narrates the brand story sincerely, celebrates corporate responsibility, and constructs a culture of respect and integrity.

Authenticity, on the other hand, involves aligning your brand's actions with its declared values. In the context of social media, it means maintaining a consistent brand voice, connecting with customers on a human level, and demonstrating empathy and understanding in all interactions. To truly master authenticity, businesses must compellingly portray their human side, crafting a brand persona that resonates with their target audience's values and concerns.

7.2. Transparency: A Cornerstone of Trust Building

Transparency in customer service operations signifies a willingness to engage in open and honest dialogue with customers. It involves actively sharing insights about the company's processes, decision-making strategies, and actions.

The origins of an effective transparency strategy lie in clear and open communication. Ensure that your communication channels, especially those on social media, are easily accessible and receptive. Cultivate an environment that encourages feedback, suggestions, and constructive criticism.

The pursuit of transparency extends towards an open admission of mistakes when problems arise. It essentially requires to avoid glossing over any issues or crises and instead taking active responsibility. Apologize sincerely if your company has slipped up and elaborate on your plan of action to rectify the situation — then do it. This demonstration of accountability can significantly enhance your brand's trustworthiness.

To further sustain transparency, endeavor to demonstrate corporate responsibility and respect for your consumers. Show how your business is adhering to ethical standards, contributing to social causes, or prioritizing environmental sustainability. This often translates into customers perceiving the brand as reliable and conscientious.

7.3. Authenticity: Embodying an Genuine Brand Persona

Authenticity in digital customer service revolves around achieving true customer engagement, accomplished by maintaining a consistent and genuine brand voice, as well as fostering empathetic interactions.

A consistent brand voice across all social media platforms signifies a reliability and singularity that customers appreciate. This voice should encapsulate your brand's vision, mission, and core values. Strive to craft your brand personality to be as humanly relatable as possible — this might involve using humor wisely, expressing empathy genuinely or celebrating your team members openly.

Connecting with customers on a deeper, emotional level solidifies the authenticity of your brand's social media presence. It allows for a genuine interaction that transcends the traditional business-customer relationship. Don't be afraid to act human — empathize with your customers, show them you understand their concerns, and work tirelessly to resolve any issues they may have.

7.4. Incorporating Transparency and Authenticity into your Strategy

To successfully integrate transparency and authenticity into your customer service strategy, precise planning and execution are vital. Start by assessing your company's current level of transparency and authenticity. How open are you with your customers? Is your brand voice consistent and relatable?

Next, invest considerable efforts in developing these facets. This often involves embedding openness and consistency into your company culture and ensuring your actions reflect these principles at every customer touchpoint. Strive to weave these characteristics into the fabric of your social media interactions.

Finally, measure the effects of your endeavors. Use social listening tools to track mentions and gauge public sentiment, analyze customer reviews for insights, and monitor your customer retention rates. By measuring these facets, you can adapt and optimize your strategy to better foster transparency and authenticity moving forward, strengthening the bonds of trust between your brand and its audience.

7.5. Conclusion

In a nutshell, the process of building trust online is a journey, not a destination. It demands constant evolution, persistently striving for transparency and authenticity in every interaction. By incorporating these principles into your digital customer service strategy, you not only enhance your relationships with customers but also boost brand loyalty, engagement, and advocacy. Traverse this journey with the understanding that successful businesses aren't just those offering great products or services — they are businesses that are trusted, relatable, transparent, and authentically engaging in the digital realms they inhabit.

Chapter 8. Engaging Through Content: Strategies for Customer Retention

In the buzzing digital landscape, it's critical to understand that content is not only a vehicle for promoting products or services but also a means to foster long-lasting customer relationships. Thoughtfully crafted and timeously delivered content can unlock new dimensions of customer engagement, setting the stage for priceless trust, loyalty, and customer retention.

8.1. The Power of Storytelling

Nothing captivates the human mind more than a compelling story. Whether it be the narrative of your brand's inception or the journey of your products from conception to completion, compelling stories instill a sense of connection and closeness in your audience. Effective storytelling can break through the noise of the digital world, penetrating deeper into the psyche of your audience. Utilizing elements of storytelling in your social media content allows you to present your business in an emotionally resonant, relatable, and human-centered manner, thereby fostering customer loyalty and retention.

Utilize posts, videos, and other content formats to spotlight behind-the-scenes processes, employee stories, success stories of other clients, and other narratives that would resonate with your audience. Be genuine and make sure the story aligns with your brand's vision and voice. Remember, customers are more likely to stick with brands that they can relate to on a personal level.

8.2. Informative and Valuable Content

With information being easily accessible, consumers are more informed than ever. They expect more than blatant promotional content from brands. This calls for a shift from a sales-focused approach to an education-based one where the primary focus is to provide valuable, relevant, and actionable information to the customer.

Ensure that your content answers potential questions customers might have about your offerings. Leverage blog posts, how-to videos, infographics, FAQ's, e-books, etc., to provide comprehensive, helpful, and expert information. Providing solutions or enlightening information that the customer genuinely needs is a sure-shot strategy for customer retention. Also, consider sharing industry news or updates that might interest your audience. This type of content entrenches your position as a thought-leader in your industry and encourages customers to trust and rely on you more often.

8.3. Interactive Content

Interactive content adds an element of engagement that can make content consumption a two-way dialogue, fostering customer adoption and retention. Social media polls, quizzes, Q&A sessions, webinars, virtual events, and user-generated content campaigns can provide customers with the opportunity to interact with your brand actively.

Customers today desire more personalized, tailored experiences. This means understanding their needs, preferences, and interests to the core and catering to them through highly personalized content. Leverage data from user behavior, feedback, previous interactions, and analytics to create content that speaks directly to individual users. This can be as simple as personalized product recommendations, tailored advice, customizable product demonstrations, or birthday wishes. Personalization in content strategy not only attracts but also entices existing customers to stay committed to your brand, thereby maximizing retention.

8.4. Consistency is Key

Undoubtedly, consistency plays a crucial role in the success of a social media content strategy. A steady stream of high-quality content not only boosts your visibility and credibility but also keeps your brand at the forefront of customers' minds, increasing the chances of customer retention.

Ensure that your content is visually consistent, maintaining a similar tone, style, and aesthetics across all content types and social media platforms. Scheduling posts regularly keeps your audience aware of your brand's presence and activities. However, strive to strike a balance to avoid over-posting, which could lead to audience fatigue and disengagement.

8.5. Measuring Content Engagement

Finally, it is vital to continually evaluate the performance of your content strategy for customer retention. This process involves understanding what content resonates with your audience, what drives engagement, and what prompts users to perform the desired actions.

Leverage social media analytics tools to measure key metrics such as post reach, shares, comments, follower count, click-through rates (CTR), and conversion rates. These insights can guide your content strategy towards more personalized, engaging, and consequently, more successful customer retention initiatives.

The journey towards excellent customer retention is a continuous process of learning, adapting, and improving. Engaging your customers through insightful, relevant, and enjoyable content fosters a relationship that goes beyond the conventional buyer-seller framework. It establishes an emotional connection, builds trust, and engenders loyalty that is the cornerstone of customer retention. As you navigate through the dynamic, often challenging realm of social media customer service, remember that content is a tool that can be powerfully wielded to retain and delight your customers. After all, in the business landscape, a satisfied customer is the best business strategy of all.

Chapter 9. Social Media Automation: Tools to Enhance Customer Service Efficiency

The insightful realization of the digital era is that the internet never sleeps, and so, your customer service ideally shouldn't either. With businesses operating across various time zones and customers expecting speedy responses, the task of addressing every query, feedback, or complaint becomes a Herculean task. Enter social media automation tools. These software applications can streamline your interactions, ensuring immediate acknowledgment of customer communications and leaving no query overlooked. By deploying these tools wisely, you can augment your customer service efficiency while weeding out the probability of human errors and inconsistencies.

9.1. The Advent of Automation in Social Media

In our technology-driven era, being able to respond instantly to customers – regardless of operating hours – is a significant competitive advantage. Automation tools, such as social media management systems and chatbots, have made it possible for businesses to stay in constant touch with their clientele without stretching human resources thin. Social media automation tools can help detect customer interactions on social platforms, categorize these interactions for relevance, and even respond with basic, automated messages. They enable brands to act swiftly, maintain a steady voice, and focus human resources where a personal touch is mandatory.

9.2. The Essentials of Social Media Automation

Integrating automation tools into your social media customer service strategy requires thoughtful planning and execution. The task involves a careful understanding of your customer needs, a well-defined response strategy and an agile approach towards refining machine responses based on feedback. Let's look at the key steps involved:

1. **Setting Up Automation**: Choosing the right automation service is critical. There are various social media customer service tools available, such as Hootsuite, Buffer, SproutSocial, etc. In setting them up, it's crucial to identify the most relevant channels your customers use, understand the tool's functionalities and customize it to match your brand's voice consistently.

2. **Defining Automation Rules**: These are guidelines that the tool will use to categorize and engage with customer interactions. It could be as simple as sending a standard reply to someone who mentions your brand on Twitter or as complex as recognising and managing negative feedback on Facebook. Clearly define these rules and parameters for the tool to optimize its benefits.

3. **Monitoring and Evolving Automation Responses**: It's nobody's argument that automation is a 'set it and forget it' solution. It requires constant refining based on customer feedback and changing business dynamics. Monitoring the performance of automation, revising pre-set responses, and making improvements are instrumental in effective social media customer service.

9.3. Key Tools for Social Media Automation

Choosing the right platforms for social media automation is an integral part of a successful customer service strategy. Here are a few leading platforms:

- **Buffer**: An intuitive social media management platform that enables businesses to streamline all of their social posts in one place. It also allows scheduling posts and examining the performance of your content.

- **Hootsuite**: A widely-used platform offering a multitude of features such as scheduling posts, tracking conversations, and managing multiple profiles. It is especially useful for large teams that need to coordinate responses.

- **SproutSocial**: A comprehensive tool that offers a range of features including scheduling, monitoring, and analytics. It also includes a dedicated CRM system, making it easy to track and manage customer conversations.

- **Zendesk**: Primarily a customer service platform, it also includes automation capabilities for managing customer support tickets generated via social media.

- **Chatfuel and ManyChat**: These platforms are used for designing and deploying chatbots on Facebook Messenger, which can be used for automating customer interactions and FAQs.

9.4. Making the Most out of Social Media Automation in Customer Service

While automation can bring about efficiencies, it must be employed astutely. Here are some additional best practices to ensure the tools add value to your customer service:

- **Maintain a Human Touch**: Striking a balance between automation and human interaction is crucial. Automation can swiftly recognize and categorize communications, but the human element is required for understanding subtleties, empathizing with customer issues and resolving complex problems.

- **Leverage Analytics**: Use the analytical capabilities of automation tools to understand customer behavior, their peak interaction times, frequently asked questions, etc. This insight can help fine-tune strategies, enhance customer engagement, and make informed business decisions.

- **Keep Your Brand Voice Consistent**: Consistency is key when communicating online. Ensure the automated replies and scheduled posts align with your company's brand voice. Inconsistencies can lead to customer confusion or mistrust.

- **Continuously Improve and Adapt**: As mentioned earlier, automation is not a 'set it and forget it' solution. Regular monitoring, learning from customer interactions, and adapting the rules and responses over time are vital to maintaining effective social media customer service.

In the modern landscape of customer service, social media automation tools offer tremendous advantages - helping businesses respond quickly, maintain consistency, and utilize resources optimally. By understanding their functionality and deploying them judiciously, businesses can significantly enhance customer service efficiency and foster robust customer relationships.

Chapter 10. Measuring Success: Analytics for Evaluating Customer Service Performance

In an epitome of business evolution, it's indisputable the vital role analytics play in assessing customer service performance. Through the kaleidoscope of comprehensive data, companies can uncover valuable insights into customer behavior, sentiment, satisfaction, and engagement. In this chapter, we delve deep into the power of analytics and how to harness it to optimize your social media customer service.

10.1. Unveiling The Power Of Analytics

Analytics works like a compass, guiding organizations through the vast ocean of data towards a more customer-centric model. Regardless of the size of your business, the potential of analytics to transform your customer service is monumental. Keep in mind: consistently augmenting customer service helps build customer loyalty, which eventually leads to increased sales, higher customer retention, and business growth.

Conventional customer service metrics, such as response time and resolution rate, are important. Still, they are only the tip of the iceberg when it comes to grasping the full extent of your performance. With social media analytics, you can dive deeper into customer interactions, revealing sentiments and trends that can drive your business strategy.

10.2. Delving Into The Metrics That Matter

There's an array of social media metrics available for evaluation. While not all are essential for every business, it's crucial to identify the handful that drive your business performance.

Response Time: This is the length of time taken to respond to a customer's query or complaint.

Satisfaction Score: Customer satisfaction score, often shortened to CSAT, illustrates the direct feedback customers provide about their service experience.

Engagement Rate: This involves the likes, shares, comments, and other actions users have taken with your posts.

- Net Promoter Score (NPS)*: This measures the willingness of customers to recommend your business to others. It's a strong indicator of customer happiness.

Sentiment Analysis: By gauging the public sentiment about your brand, you can better position your messaging.

Conversion Rate: The rate at which customer interactions lead to a predefined goal, such as a purchase, signup, or download.

10.3. Taming The Data Beast: Tools For Analytics

To harness the dynamism of these metrics, a repertoire of tools exists. With a variety of price points and capabilities, tools like Hootsuite, Google Analytics, Sprout Social, and others offer in-depth insights into customer behavior on social media. However, the most effective customer service is one that employs a combination of these tools, offering a broader understanding of your brand's online engagement.

10.4. Interpreting Analytics: From Insights to Action

Interpreting analytics is more of an art than a science. Here, you give meaning to the numbers, transforming raw data into actionable strategies. Regular analysis of the identified metrics will reveal actionable patterns that can be used to improve customer service. Patterns might indicate which content generates the most positive reactions, what time of day customers are most active, or common complaints among customers.

Remember, interpretation is only valuable if it leads to implementation. For example, if analytics reveal an increase in complaints during a particular time of day, set out a plan to increase customer service personnel during these peak hours. Act upon this new knowledge - that is true power of analytics!

Analyzing performance is not a one-time task but a continuous effort. It's a cycle of setting goals, measuring performance, interpreting results, implementing changes, and then measuring again. As we continue to adapt to the fast-paced digital landscape, more sophisticated metrics will emerge. Being prepared to evolve with these changes is essential to sustain success.

10.5. The Path Forward

Analytics is continually evolving, as are customer expectations. Stay ahead of the curve by investing in the right tools and people to analyze your social media performance properly. Track your metrics, interpret your data, and act on those insights - these are the keys to a successful social media customer service strategy.

In essence, effective use of analytics can be a game-changer in elevating the quality of your customer service. By making informed decisions, you can cultivate a loyal customer base, improve customer experience, and ultimately drive business growth in the flourishing realm of entrepreneurship. The magic lies in mastering the art of converting facts and data into action and embracing the power of continuous learning and adaptation.

Chapter 11. Sustaining Growth: Adapting Customer Service in the Age of Change

In the ever-evolving digital landscape, maintaining a growth trajectory with altering customer service dynamics is a challenge no entrepreneur can escape. The keen necessity to adapt, the impetus to innovate, and the constant drive towards improvement mark the journey of sustainable growth in today's volatile market.

11.1. Recognizing the Fluid Nature of Trends

Digitalization has revolutionized customer service experiences. It has propelled businesses into a state of constant recalibration as new technologies and social mediation practices emerge. These technological tools and platforms transform customers' expectations, making it imperative for businesses to stay abreast. Trend forecasting models can be employed to anticipate changes and build resilience. This adaptability can foster sustainable growth as customer experiences continue to influence success in the social media arena.

11.2. Embracing Artificial Intelligence and Automation

Artificial Intelligence (AI) and automation have vastly enhanced the capabilities of social media customer service. Mass responses can be automated, customer inquiries can be organized methodically, and valuable customer data can be analyzed for insightful business strategies. Businesses can employ AI-powered chatbots for automated responses, sentiment analysis for precise customer feedback interpretation, or machine learning algorithms for predictive customer behavior modeling.

11.3. Learning from Customer Data Analytics

Analytics is an invaluable tool that offers multiple layers of customer comprehension. Analyzing patterns present in customer feedback, interaction frequency, and response satisfaction rates provides businesses with the pulse of their customer base. This data can reveal what works, what doesn't, and where improvements are needed. It can drive modification of tactics, ensuring that businesses are not just responding to changes, but also proactively shaping their customer service narratives.

11.4. Exploring Newer Social Media Platforms

The digital domain is characterized by an ever-expanding list of social media platforms. As target customers switch from one platform to another, businesses need to create a presence across a variety of social channels while maintaining a consistent brand image. Being versatile on multiple platforms not only helps reach a more significant segment of customers but also enables businesses to customize their customer service based on each platform's unique characteristics.

11.5. Enhancing Personalization through Technology

Tech enables businesses to bring personalization to unprecedented levels. Personalization, a key driver of customer satisfaction, can form the cornerstone of a dynamic customer service strategy. Analytical tools can help businesses understand customer preferences at an individual level, enabling them to serve the customer better and forge deeper connections. Customized messages and suggestions based on previous interactions, buying history, and recent searches can create a unique customer journey.

11.6. Upholding Ethical Digital Practices

Respecting privacy and practicing transparency should underline a business's online operations. With the increased adoption of digital services and data analytics, businesses find themselves custodians of an overwhelming amount of customer data. Privacy breaches risk undermining customer trust and causing significant reputational damage. Prioritization of ethical practices and commitment to data protection not only meets legal obligations but also fosters an atmosphere of trust, critical for long-term customer relationships.

11.7. Preparing for Crisis Management

Online platforms, while empowering businesses, can also pose significant threats. A single negative remark can snowball into a crisis situation. Companies should have a crisis management plan that includes specific steps to tactfully handle sudden negative publicity, communicate effectively with customers during crises, and mitigate potential damage.

11.8. Fostering an Agile Customer Service Culture

The final and perhaps the most crucial aspect is developing an agile culture within the organization. Companies that value flexibility, quick decision-making, and continuous learning are better adapted to an ever-changing digital landscape. Encouraging employees to acquire new skills, investing in their development, and fostering a culture that values innovation over bureaucratic decision-making can empower businesses to sustain growth in the face of change.

In conclusion, sustaining growth while adapting customer service dynamics in this digital age necessitates constant innovation, adaptability, and a commitment to learning. Understanding changes, implementing new technologies, respecting customer privacy, and nurturing a flexible organizational culture are the key proponents of a successful social media customer service strategy. The journey may continually pose challenges, but with every hurdle overcome, businesses solidify their foundation in the intricately connected world of social media customer service.